The Pastel Pets
of
Ms. Patty Pummill

Illustrated
by
Grace Obenhaus

Story by Rick Mansfield

The Pastel Pets of Ms. Patty Pummill

This book is fiction, as are all the characters. The Bible quotations are quite real and worthy of study. Recipes in back are old-family recipes handed down through several generations.

Dedication

This book is dedicated to all those who find themselves struggling with new challenges and nursing old hurts. To all those in pain and dealing with fears; whatever their age or station in life. To all those who go out of their way to ease their burdens and inspire them to find both strength and talent within themselves.

We hope and pray these words and especially these pictures lighten loads and enlighten hearts. May this book cause the reader to see the world in a more beautiful and serene way. May it cause both laughter and lightheartedness in all!

Acknowledgments

I remain thankful for my wife and helpmate, Judy; whose love and support make my writing possible. Thankful for the Lord and Savior who inspires and guides me; for His love as well as the myriad of blessings I so often receive.

I am thankful for His providence that brought the Obenhaus family into my life. It was their desire to see this book in print, their collaborative effort on so many of the elements of the story, and Grace's wonderful artwork that made this book possible.

It was as a family that shared ideas completed this work and have helped outline the series. Visit examples of their work at Facebook *Heritage Arrows.*

Once again, I thank Phyliss of Minit Print for her work on the back cover. Always quality work and friendly service.

I remain thankful for the child within that still sees the occasional dinosaur or woolly mammoth in a cloud on a summer day; the magic and wonder of a field of fireflies at night. This book, especially the pictures, capture much of that feeling. Please enjoy!

"And He said: 'Truly I tell you, unless you change and become like little children, you will never enter the kingdom of Heaven.'"

Matthew 18:3

Patty was feeling lonely. Very lonely. Lonely as only a young girl in a strange new home in a strange new town could feel.

The home was really neither strange nor new. In fact, it seemed to be an ordinary house, much like she had seen in family photographs. And it was certainly not new. In fact, it appeared quite old. Much like the woman who ran the house. The woman whom she was to call Granny Gail.

Circumstances at home had brought about this recent change. Hope of better times ahead had led to the promise "It's only for the summer."

So, here she was. No friends. School was out and there was nothing to do. No one even walked down the sidewalk by their old house, as years of freezing and thawing had separated the slabs into quite an uneven pathway.

In the evening she read, as Granny Gail had no television; no video games. Due to their current hardships, Patty no longer had her cell phone. Once a week her mother called on Granny Gail's land line.

It was during the warm, sunny days she believed she had nothing to do. She began to almost dread the rising of the sun; knowing it gave way to the long, lonely afternoons.

Still, Granny Gail insisted Patty "go outside and play." Often while the older guardian took a nap.

One day Granny Gail told Patty she had a surprise. There, on the table side a platter of elderberry "blo" pancakes and just beyond her daily glass of orange juice was an old cigar box. She smiled at the *White Owl* logo.

Surely, Patty wondered, she was not about to be encouraged to take up smoking? Urged to "go ahead and open it", Patty found herself looking at lots of different little colored sticks. They were just about the size of her ring finger, in both length and circumference.

"They were my pastel chalks in high school" Granny Gail was explaining. "I used them to draw pictures on that sidewalk out front. Drew my first picture not much more than a week after the city finished and the concrete dried."

After a few brief lessons, where Granny Gail taught Patty to use different shapes to form the various body parts of animals; Patty was directed outside.

She tried drawing a square and then a circle. Finally, picking up the blue piece of chalk, she drew a pretty fair oval. She -re-positioned herself on the old piece of concrete and added a circle on top. Two more skinny ovals on top of that and she had ears. Then some round eyes and a small triangle for a nose.

She added some big back legs and feet and there before her was a bunny rabbit. A bright blue bunny. She named it Bobby. Bobby the Blue Bunny!

At first, she had trouble believing how lifelike Bobby looked. He almost seemed alive. So much so she began to speak to him.

After a few moments, Patty noticed that Bobby was speaking back! It began with a subtle "Mmmm" and then evolved into "Yes, I agree" as she had just commented on the beauty of the sky.

Patty enjoyed her new friend and hurried out after breakfast the next day to resume their much-enjoyed conversation. After a bit, the bunny rabbit asked Patty "Am I your only friend?"

Patty thought. "Yes. I guess now you are. Am I yours? Or do you have other friends?"

"I have one I haven't seen for a while. We met in a farmer's field while dining. I was enjoying the smaller white clover; he relished the taller red clover. And dandelions. Gary loved dandelions. We got along fine."

"What was his name?" Patty inquired.

"Gary. He's a groundhog. Sometimes he was hard to see in the field; because, well Gary is green."

"Gary the Green Groundhog" mused Patty. She got her chalk and began to draw. A couple of circles, a fuzzy sided rectangle and the slightly jade woodchuck began to take shape.

"Is this how he looked?" asked Patty.

"Maybe a bit taller" was the polite reply.

Soon, there on the sidewalk was a green outline of a groundhog. Moments later there was Gary!

"How do you do?" asked the little mammal. By now, Patty was no longer surprised.

"Fine, thank you" Patty responded. "And you must be Bobby's friend Gary."

"I do have that honor" he said, while turning towards the rabbit. "Bobby, how have you been? Visited any good clover fields lately?"

Patty sat and listened to them visit. The sun's rays warm on her face; she closed her eyes. The next thing she knew, she had drifted off to sleep. When she awoke, both Gary and Bobby were gone.

For the next two days, she did not see either of her new friends. Friday afternoon, she played Tic-Tac-Toe by herself. She even used two different colors of chalk to try and pretend she was not alone. She continued to hope they would reappear. Her mother made her weekly call earlier than usual and Patty missed it.

That night, while feeling kind of sad, Patty began to sing. Singing always made her happy. She sang softly so as not to disturb her grandmother. Patty sang "The Crawdad Song." It was an old tune her mother taught her years ago. Finally, she drifted off to sleep.

The following day, after a breakfast of now elderberry pancakes, Granny Gail suggested Patty leave her chalk box behind and "run an errand." She was to take a pair of scissors and an emptied glass milk jar now a third full of water and "go gather some wildflowers to decorate this old house!"

Taking a path that Granny Gail had told her led to an old mill pond, Patty walked through a field of fringed orchid and wood lilies. They varied in height and ranged from bright yellow to soft shades of peach. As she neared the pond, she passed a glade of purple cone flowers.

When Patty got back to her house (she now thought of the old house as her home), Granny Gail was setting out lunch on the front porch. Patty placed the makeshift vase on the table and went inside to wash her hands. When she returned outside, there was one of her favorite meals. Grilled cheese sandwiches and homemade tomato soup. The day was a bit overcast and the warm meal really hit the spot.

"Why don't you get your chalks and draw some while I clean up" her grandmother suggested.

Patty went to her room, got the old cigar box and headed back outside. When she opened the box, and began rummaging through the different pieces of chalk, she noticed a slip of brown parchment she did not recall ever seeing before.

The excursion outside. Her favorite meal. Now this. Patty suspected that maybe her grandmother had heard her singing last night, after all.

"*This is the day which the Lord hath made; we will rejoice and be glad in it.*" Psalm 118:24

Smiling, she began to draw. It almost seemed like her hand had a mind of its own. Soon, there beside her earlier drawings was an armadillo and a muskrat. The armadillo was apricot and the muskrat magenta.

Patty laughed! How real these new characters looked! While she was thinking this, the muskrat said hello. Not to her, but to the armadillo.

"Howdy right back at you" the banded critter returned with a somewhat sweet Southern drawl. "I'm April."

"I'm Maggie. Who's the artist?" As she said this, the magenta muskrat looked towards Patty; as did April the apricot armadillo.

"Why, I'm Patty. Patty Pummill. I don't know that you could accurately call me an artist. I draw a little."

"You did a fine job with us" continued April the apricot armadillo.

"Second that!" concurred Maggie the magenta muskrat.

"Well, we can all thank my Granny Gail" explained Patty. "It was Granny Gail who gave me her old chalks and got me started."

"Gail, you say" questioned April, the apricot armadillo. Patty nodded.

"But you called her Granny Gail?" asked Maggie, the magenta muskrat.

"Yes!" maintained Patty. "Granny Gail is my grandmother. My mother's mother. I have always called her 'Granny Gail.'"

The muskrat and armadillo exchanged a knowing glance but said no more. Quickly, the armadillo changed the subject.

"To whom should a critter smile to get a glass of sweet tea. I swallowed some ants a while ago and I need something with which to wash them down" April drawled in what could only be described as a charmingly fetching tone.

After all had had some sweet tea, as well as quite a bit of conversation, the warm sun again put Patty to sleep. And once again, when she awoke, her newest companions were gone.

The warm days of late spring became the hot days of midsummer. Patty had not seen any of her pastel friends recently. She had remained quite busy in her grandmother's garden. There were green beans to pick and can; tomatoes from which they made salsa and soup base. Sweet corn with which they made relish and then field corn to be picked, shelled and stored for "feeding the critters" during the coming winter.

Patty continued to draw. Mostly landscapes and many of the old structures around town. She drew people's houses. She drew old barns, some still in use. She did a nice landscape of the mill pond, capturing a few of the rocks that had long ago been part of the mill's foundation.

Patty also continued to find those "new" old slips of parchment. Always one to pray before meals and at bedtime, she now found herself thinking about the different verses of scripture each time a new treasure was discovered in the cigar box.

Favorites included Romans 8:31, ***"What then shall we say to these things? If God is for us, who can be against us?"*** This passage gave her strength when the challenges before she and her mother seemed so great. Most weeks she was present for her mother's one call, and she often shared her newest "treasure" from the chalk box. This particular one made her mother glad, as she said when Patty finished reading it.

Another favorite was 1 Timothy 4:12. ***"Let no one despise you for your youth, but set the believers an example in speech, in conduct, in love, in faith, in purity."*** Though from her study, she knew that the young ministerial agent of Paul's was much older than she when this was directed to him. She knew also that Timothy had been but a teenager when he first began assisting the apostle. Maybe not that much older than she herself was now.

Though the isolation of the town during the summer and the solitude of her Granny Gail's life led to few interactions, Patty strived to truly live the directives of that verse.

Patty also continued to sing. Not so often in the evenings, she did not want to cause Granny Gail undo distress. Mostly while doing chores or walking through the woods and around town. Whenever she was sad and alone. She sang many of the tunes she remembered her mother teaching her, but always seemed to return to the Crawdad Song.

Summer had given way to fall. Each burst of wind contained a bit more of chill and a new offering of falling leaves. Patty added drawing the many different shapes and colors of these to her curriculum. School had already begun, but Granny Gail was teaching her at home for the "time being." Drawing on the sidewalk was now as much homework as recreation.

The garden was finally winding down; chores becoming fewer each day. It was while checking the pumpkin patch that Patty first noticed the series of raised earth running through the edge of the garden. She stepped on one of the elevated lines and immediately heard "Ouch!"

Patty jumped off and back. "I am sorry" she instinctively offered. "Are you okay?"

"I think so" came a diminutive reply from somewhere under the earth. The sod had fallen in and a bit of a hole was visible; through which Patty saw something amazing! Patty called out to whatever it was several more times, but to no avail. As soon as she finished her chores, she retrieved her box of chalks and headed to the sidewalk.

She wasn't quite drawing from memory, for she had only got a glimpse. As she drew, another of her treasures came to mind. It was in Matthew, she believed chapter 13. The parable of the four soils. Though so much scripture directed her to "look above", she liked this one because it reinforced the importance of what was beneath us. On what type of ground we wished to stand.

As much as she had enjoyed watching things grow this summer, Patty was again reminded to look down. Just as she had looked down to dig potatoes. To gather beets and turnips. Now she tried to "look down" and capture the image of what she had so briefly seen.

Patty's hand seemed to decide by itself which color of chalk to use; the shapes seemed to form on their own. Unlike her previous experiences with the armadillo and muskrat, even the bunny—she had no idea what the creature was that now lay before her.

Like the "good soil" of which Matthew wrote, she was certain there was something important to be found here. Patty thoughtfully pondered the questions. What had she seen? What was she missing? Closing her eyes, she silently prayed for answers.

"My name is Veronica. What's yours?"

Patty opened her eyes. There before her, at the edge of the yard was the living embodiment of what she'd been trying to draw.

"I'm Patty. Patty Pummill. What are you?" the young girl asked of the new creature she saw before her. A beautiful violet creature the likes of which she had never seen before. It stood timidly near one of the first acorns to have fallen this year.

"I'm a vole. A friendly vole. I eat the larvae of gypsy moths, so they don't grow up and kill your trees. Bye now!" And just like that, she was gone.

Patty did not wish to lose another friend. Now having gotten a better look, she redrew the violet creature. She had no more than finished shading in the sketch than she heard "Well, hello again, Ms. Patty Pummill."

This creature was a bit more soft spoken than its predecessors. She was also more shy; or so it appeared.

After a bit more conversation, first of the weather and then about the color of the squash on trellises nearby; Patty risked asking this latest apparition what she had been wondering now for months.

"Why do you all disappear so suddenly? And why don't you come back?"

"I came back" Veronica the violet vole answered sweetly. "And there's your answer." With that, she was gone again.

This time Patty decided that her second drawing had been close, but the eyes needed to be closer together. Closer together and a wee bit darker. Almost black. She set to drawing.

"Yes. That's it. Now you have it. Now draw Bobby and Gary and the rest!" urged Veronica. With such explicit encouragement, Patty began drawing. Soon, there sat Gary with a sprig of clover in his paws, dandelion season now long past. Bobby was close by, and then with a few more strokes of her chalk---April.

"I do say, how about that tea? That is, if it would not be too much of a bother" the apricot armadillo drawled enchantingly.

"Just a few more seconds. Almost done" Patty reported as she finished the last of her sketches. "I'll go get us all some tea" she announced without bothering to look back; confident that a magenta muskrat was making her presence known in the rapidly crowding yard.

After they had all had their tea, and everyone was well reacquainted; Patty asked again.

"Where did you all go this summer. I missed you!"

"We were always here" explained Veronica, the newest of the set. "We come whenever you call us. You call us by drawing us on this old sidewalk."

"That's all it takes?" Patty asked, somewhat surprised.

"'That's all' she asks" laughed Maggie, the magenta muskrat. "That's a lot!"

"That doesn't seem like so very much. Just a chalk drawing on an old broken-down sidewalk" Patty countered.

"It's so much more than that" Veronica continued to explain. "First, you have to see us. In your mind. In your heart. Then you have to wish so hard that you believe. That is what brings us back. Will bring us all back."

"And the singing" contributed Bobby, the blue bunny. "I like the singing."

Patty had listened carefully, as her mother had taught her. As her Granny Gail always reminded her.

"All of you? Are there more?" Patty was excited and curious, and not a little bit apprehensive.

"What do you see?" responded Veronica. April and Maggie nodded in agreement to the violet vole's response; while Bobby and Gary just smiled.

Later, ecstatic and exhausted; Patty went to bed. And to sleep. She awoke in the middle of the night. She had sought answers below and found Veronica. Found the secret to calling her friends at will. She remembered the treasure that had been in the box just that evening.

James 1:17. *"Every good and perfect gift is from above…."*

Patty put on a robe and ventured outside, careful not to wake her grandmother. It was a full moon. A harvest moon, so called because in times gone by farmers used the extra light to get in an abundant crop. She wandered out into the yard.

There, silhouetted against the orange globe dominating the night sky, was North America's only marsupial. The ends of its light-colored fur almost incandescent in the moonlight, there it sat on a limb in a persimmon tree. Patty immediately went back to her room and gathered her chalks.

She said a little prayer as she started to draw. She created the outline, using shapes very much as she had when she first drew Bobby, the blue bunny. She sketched the trunk of the persimmon tree, and the limb upon which it sat. She blended some white with red to get the colors just right. Then she returned to the persimmon tree.

The smile looking down at her put her in mind of Carroll's famous feline. "How do you do?" Patty offered in way of salutation.

"Just fine!" came the reply. "Yourself?"

"Awed and awesome!" was Patty's happy response back. "Why don't you come down" the girl continued.

"Maybe tomorrow. Tonight, I like it up here. I also like that people have to look up to see me!"

"You enjoy being a star?" Patty asked.

"I'm no star. No, when people have to look up they then see so much more than me."

"The moon is sure enough pretty" agreed Patty.

"That it is!" agreed the climbing critter. "Well worth dwelling on. But I wish you to really dwell on is what is beyond that. The Creator of that moon. And this tree of ripe fruit. And, well, even me. Priscilla."

"All good things......" remembered Patty. "All good things."

They visited a bit longer; the young girl and the friendly marsupial. After a while, Patty was beginning to become quite cool and bid goodnight to her newest friend. "See you in the morning" she promised.

Priscilla had been right. While looking up at the tree and its occupant, while looking at the beautiful autumn moon; her thoughts turned to He who had created it all. As she turned towards the house, Patty said a silent prayer for herself and for her family.

"Amen" came from the branch of the tree as Patty walked in.

Over the next few days, Patty drew all six of her new friends after breakfast each morning. As she drew them on the aging sidewalk each day shortly after sunrise; they all came to life. Bobby the Blue Bunny. Gary the Green Groundhog. Maggie the Magenta Muskrat. April the Apricot Armadillo and Veronica the Violet Vole. And always last, but certainly not least---Priscilla the Pink Possum.

That next Friday there was no call from her mother. Patty drew her friends. Played hopscotch and tic-tac-toe. And sang. That evening she sang. But before she went to sleep, she did not just pray. She looked up and spoke to God. Spoke as she would to a trusting father no longer present. Patty made both promises and requests; the latter mostly for her mother and her grandmother. And she gave Him thanks for all the good things in her life. Patty slept very soundly that night.

The next morning she slept later than usual. When she came downstairs for breakfast, there were three plates on the table. And sitting in the chair nearest the stove was her mother!

With tears forming in her eyes, she ran to give her a hug. Meanwhile her Granny Gail was explaining "when the letter came a few days ago, I didn't want to get your hopes up……something might have happened….but here she is."

The sweet potato pancakes they had that morning seemed especially delicious. The bacon had that "just right" amount of crispness. After the meal, and after the dishes were washed and put away; they all three went outside.

"Oh, wait just a minute. I'll be right back!" Patty excused herself and ran back upstairs to her room. Returning with the old cigar box full of chalk, she kneeled down on the sidewalk. "You won't believe what you're about to see. Just watch."

As Patty began to draw, the mother looked at her daughter, then at Granny Gail—her own mother. She then spoke to her daughter, who was beginning to draw.

She asked the question with great love. "Which critter did you meet first?"

Bonus Section

We hope that you have enjoyed the first in this seven-book series, and that you will end up collecting them all. To extend that enjoyment now, following are some enrichment activities that will enable you to dig deeper into perhaps thoughts invoked and dreams inspired by these wonderful drawings.

The reader and family can work through some of the learning opportunities concerning the scripture referenced in the story. This book is being published with the intention of Honoring our Lord and inspiring others to develop the relationship He would have us all enjoy. Activities are also designed to promote the positive interaction of family members.

We begin with five lessons based on scripture embedded within the story. Challenges range from the recognition of facts to the creation and evaluation of plans to implement in their own lives based on God's word. We have included some ideas on things to draw, as that is an important part of a child's creative process. For the drawing activities, simple graphite or colored pencils or crayons will suffice. Or even chalk!

The section concludes with recipes of meals mentioned in the story, including two of Patty's favorite dishes—grilled cheese sandwiches and homemade tomato soup. Depending on the age and skills of the child, older siblings and/or parents can either monitor or assist the reader in their preparation. In this section, the colloquialism "elderberry blo" is explained.

Then the family can sit together and enjoy the meal. Meals begun with a prayer and that include opportunity for those present to share whatever recent blessings they've enjoyed. Have a pleasant day and may God Bless you and yours. Thanks for joining us!

Activity One

"This is the day which the Lord hath made; we will rejoice and be glad in it."

Psalm 118:24

1) Is this passage found in the Old or the New Testament?

2) Where did Patty find the written scripture?

3) On what type of material was the passage written?

4) Immediately following the passage of scripture, the book mentions an "excursion." Where did that excursion take place and what was the task assigned by Granny Gail?

5) What dishes composed her "favorite meal" also mentioned there?

6) Which animals did the experience inspire Patty to draw?

7) What do you think inspired each animal specifically?

8) Close your eyes and imagine walking along some favored pathway. What do you recall the best?

9) If you were to draw something based on that memory and experience, what would you most likely draw?

10) What is one way that you can "rejoice and be glad" in every day?

11) Draw something for which you are grateful.

Activity Two

"What then shall we say to these things? If God is for us, who can be against us?"

1) Besides the "pastel pets" what other things did Patty draw?

2) What were some challenges Patty was having to deal with that summer?

3) What are some challenges you deal with? Homework? Chores?

4) Ever feel like "the world is against you?" What do you do when you feel that way?

5) Is there anyone or anything more powerful than God?

6) When troubled, to whom do you turn? A parent? A close friend?

7) When do you pray?

8) How can praying to God give us strength?

9) What are some examples in the Bible of God helping someone in desperate need?

10) Draw someone in the Bible being helped by God.

Activity Three

"Let no one despise you for your youth, but set the believers an example in speech, in conduct, in love, in faith, in purity."

I Timothy 4:12

1) Who are some people that have been good examples in your life?

2) What specific things did they do to set this good example?

3) Which people for whom do you set examples? Younger siblings? Schoolmates?

4) What things do you do that would be good examples to follow?

5) What behaviors do you possibly do occasionally that would be bad examples to follow?

6) How might you change, decrease or eliminate those behaviors?

7) Of the traits listed---speech, conduct, love, faith and purity—which do you believe the most difficult to control?

8) Who is an example of a Bible "hero" displaying one of these traits?

9) Patty tried to exemplify her best behaviors in these areas. Why is it more difficult for youth to do so?

10) Draw one of these traits, or something that reminds you of one.

Activity Four

"Still other seed fell on good soil, where it produced a crop-----a hundred, sixty or thirty times what was sown."

Matthew 13: 8

1) Where did the other seeds fall?   Three parts to this answer.

   a.

   b.

   c.

2)   What is a parable?

3) Why do you believe Jesus so often used parables to make a point?

4) Do you have a favorite parable from the New Testament?

5) What had Patty seen that made her think of this particular parable?

6) What can we do to keep from losing a friend?

7) Plant a bean seed in a small container with good soil and watch it grow.

8) Go outside and look at a small patch of ground; roughly the size of a sheet of paper. What all do you see?

9) How is "soil" comparable to our heart?

10) Draw a picture of one of the four types of soil of which the parable spoke.

Activity Five

"Every good and perfect gift is from above……."

James 1:17

1) Why were some full moons called "harvest moons?"

2) What activities have you done under moonlight? Gone for a walk? Sat beside a stream?

3) What was the "above" the scripture Patty read speaking about?

4) When you look up into the night sky, what do you most like to see?

5) Have you ever looked up at daytime sky and thought about what animals the clouds look like?

6) What are some of the "good and perfect" gifts we receive from above?

7) What are some that you personally have received?

8) If not perfect, what are some "good" gifts we can give to others?

9) Go outside and close your eyes at night; then open them slowly. How much can you see looking up into the sky?

10) Draw a scene of the outdoors under a full moon, or a picture of the sky with the moon in it.

Elderberry Blo Pancakes

"Blo" was the term used in the Shannon County homes where I grew up, referring to the "blossoms" or the flowers of the elderberry plant. Below is how to prepare them with any good pancake recipe. We have included an old favorite.

1) Harvest blossoms by shaking the clusters in a clean paper bag, or over a large clean container. Be sure the flowers are fresh and white, NOT brown. Rinse and clean them, discarding discolored blossoms, woody stems and leaves. Wrap flowers in a towel to absorb excess water while you prepare pancake batter,

2) Pancake batter ingredients
   a. 2 cups of flour
   b. 2 tablespoons sugar
   c. 2 teaspoons baking powder
   d. ½ teaspoon baking soda
   e. 2 cups buttermilk (or 2 cups milk plus 1 tablespoon lemon juice)
   f. 1 large egg
   g. 3 tablespoons unsalted butter, melted and slightly cooled
   h. Oil for skillet (cast iron cookware works great)

3) Making the batter
   a. Combine dry ingredients in a large bowl, wisk together and then form a well in the middle. Set aside and combine all wet ingredients in small bowl and wisk together.
   b. Pour wet ingredients into the well you formed in dry ingredients. Wisk together, but let batter remain somewhat lumpy. The batter will be thick. Do not cover.
   c. Add elderberry blossoms, with only what stirring is needed to distribute.

4) Heat a couple of tablespoons of olive oil (bacon grease also tastes great) in flat-bottomed skillet. Not too hot.

5) Pour ¼ to ½ of mixture into skillet once oil is hot. Might have to lightly press on batter to make it flatten out. Tilt skillet as needed to allow oil to cover skillet. Cook about 2 minutes and then flip to brown the other side; not quite as long.

You can keep pancakes warm in oven if necessary. Serve with butter and even elderberry syrup. Make elderberry pancakes the same way, only add clean berries in place of the blossoms. Both types are delicious, and both types of pancakes may be made with your favorite recipe, even an instant batter mix.

Grilled Cheese

Ingredients

    2 tablespoons canola oil

    8 (1 0z) whole wheat bread slices

    3 ounces thinly sliced fresh mozzarella cheese

    1 ½ ounces (1/3 cup) shredded Monterey Jack cheese

Step 1

Brush canola oil evenly over I side of whole-wheat bread slices. Arrange 4 slices oiled side down on a work surface. Divide mozzarella cheese and Monterey Jack cheese evenly among bread slices; top each with another bread slice, oiled side up.

Step 2

Cook sandwiches in large skillet over medium-high until toasted and cheese is melted—about three minutes on each side.

Old-Fashioned Creamy Tomato Soup

Ingredients

    2 tablespoons butter

    1 onion, chopped

    2 tablespoons all-purpose flour

    1 quart tomato juice (Granny Gail uses juice canned from her own garden)

    Salt to taste

    2 cups milk

Preparation

In a Dutch oven, over medium heat, sauté onions in butter until translucent. Remove from heat. Stir in the flour so that no lumps remain, then slowly whisk in the tomato juice. Return to the heat and add salt to taste. Cook until just boiling but turn off the heat before it boils. Let cool 10 minutes then slowly stir in milk. Serve immediately.

The Crawdad Song

F

You get a line I'll get a pole, honey

F   C

You get a line I'll get a pole, babe

F

You get a line I'll get a pole,

G#

We'll go down to the crawdad hole

F   C   F

Honey, baby, mine

Made in the USA
Columbia, SC
08 July 2018